THE ROANOKE, JAMESTOWN AND WILLIAMSBURG COLONIES

Colonial America History Book 5Th Grade | Children's American History

BABY PROFESSOR
EDUCATION KIDS

Speedy Publishing LLC
40 E. Main St. #1156
Newark, DE 19711
www.speedypublishing.com
Copyright 2017

All Rights reserved. No part of this book may be reproduced or used in any way or form or by any means whether electronic or mechanical, this means that you cannot record or photocopy any material ideas or tips that are provided in this book.

In this book, we're going to talk about the American colonies of Roanoke, Jamestown, and Williamsburg. So, let's get right to it!

It wasn't until Christopher Columbus sailed across the Atlantic Ocean in 1492 that the Europeans realized there were two huge continents located an ocean away from them. It was almost a century later when Europeans began to travel to the New World to find their fortunes, explore, establish towns, and eventually create a new country.

The Landing of Columbus

THE LOST COLONY OF ROANOKE

Ninety-two years after Christopher Columbus sailed to America, in the year 1584, Queen Elizabeth I gave the land of Virginia to Raleigh. The British people wanted to expand their territories by establishing colonies for the kingdom in the New World. Raleigh sent two experienced captains on an expedition to find a suitable location for a colony.

They picked Roanoke Island, which was part of the land of Virginia at that time, but is now considered to be part of North Carolina.

Roanoke map

THE FIRST COLONY AT ROANOKE

A year later, Sir Richard Greenville sailed with over 100 men to the site and left them there under the leadership of Ralph Lane. Sir Richard then returned to England to obtain additional supplies that the colony needed. The settlers constructed a fort for defense for they were constantly engaging in battle with the local natives.

Statue to Sir Francis Drake

They were struggling to stay alive in the New World and were desperate to leave. When Sir Francis Drake, the English explorer, arrived with his ships, they begged to go back to England. When Greenville came back with his supplies and some additional men, he realized the colonists had left. A few men stayed at Roanoke while Greenville headed back to England.

THE SECOND COLONY AT ROANOKE

In 1587, John White traveled to Roanoke with a group of 115 new settlers. They hoped to be met by the men that they knew had been left on the island. However, when they got there the scene was not what they expected. They found some human remains, but no one was there.

John White

Roanoke Tribe

Soon, just as before, the new group of settlers were struggling too. The environment was harsh and fights with the natives were frequent. White knew they would need supplies and more manpower so he left for England to secure additional help.

England was in the midst of a war with Spain when White returned there. It took him three years to go back to Roanoke. When he and the additional men got there, there was no one there. The site had been completely abandoned. He had told the settlers to carve a symbol of a Maltese cross if they were forced to abandon the site.

Maltese Cross

No such carving was found. The only thing he found was the etching "Croatoan" carved into a piece of a wooden fencepost and the shorter "Cro" etched into a tree bark.

The word could have meant a nearby island or the name of the Native Americans who lived there. To this day no one knows what happened to the people of the Roanoke colony. Archaeologists and historians are still trying to piece together clues to uncover the mystery of what happened.

Archaeologists working in field

THE JAMESTOWN COLONY

The settlement of Jamestown was established in the year 1607. It was the first North American settlement inhabited by people from England that survived. England's king, James I, offered the Virginia Company the opportunity to begin a colony. Wealthy English gentlemen bought stock in the company in the hopes that once the colony was started it would turn a profit either in agriculture or industry.

The settlement had a rough start, but eventually it would become the capital city of the Virginia colony and would remain the capital for more than 80 years.

Cape Henry Lighthouse in Virginia

TRAVELING TO AMERICA

The company sent out an expedition that included over 140 men. They set sail in three separate ships in December of 1606 and traveled across the Atlantic Ocean. They landed in what is now Puerto Rico to get fresh supplies and then headed north along the coast of America. It took them four months after they left England to arrive in Virginia at Cape Henry.

THE POWHATAN

Soon after the English settlers arrived, they discovered that there were Native Americans living in the area that were part of a large group of tribes. At first the natives were hostile and violent. They captured and killed some of the settlers, so the settlers were afraid of them.

Powhatan Tribe

Settlers building the fort

THE JAMESTOWN FORT

The settlers needed to construct a fort so that they could defend themselves if the natives or other Europeans attacked them. They traveled up and down the coast and then decided on an island location. They thought that with the addition of the fort, the island would be easy to defend. They constructed the fort in a triangular shape and named their new settlement Jamestown after the king.

Unfortunately, they had made a poor selection in terms of location. In the winter, the island had very intense, cold storms and during the summer, the land turned very marshy and mosquitoes swarmed there.

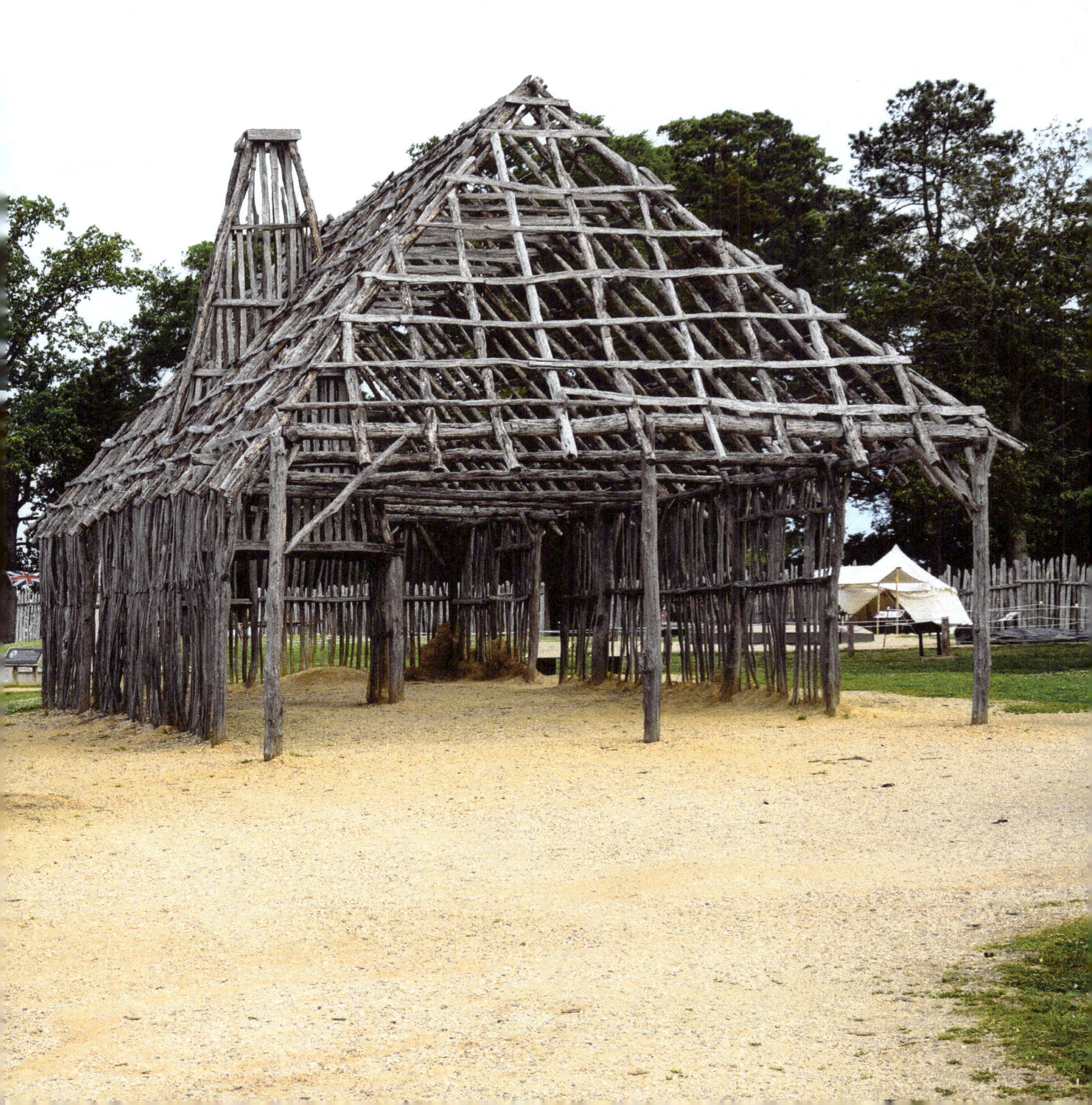

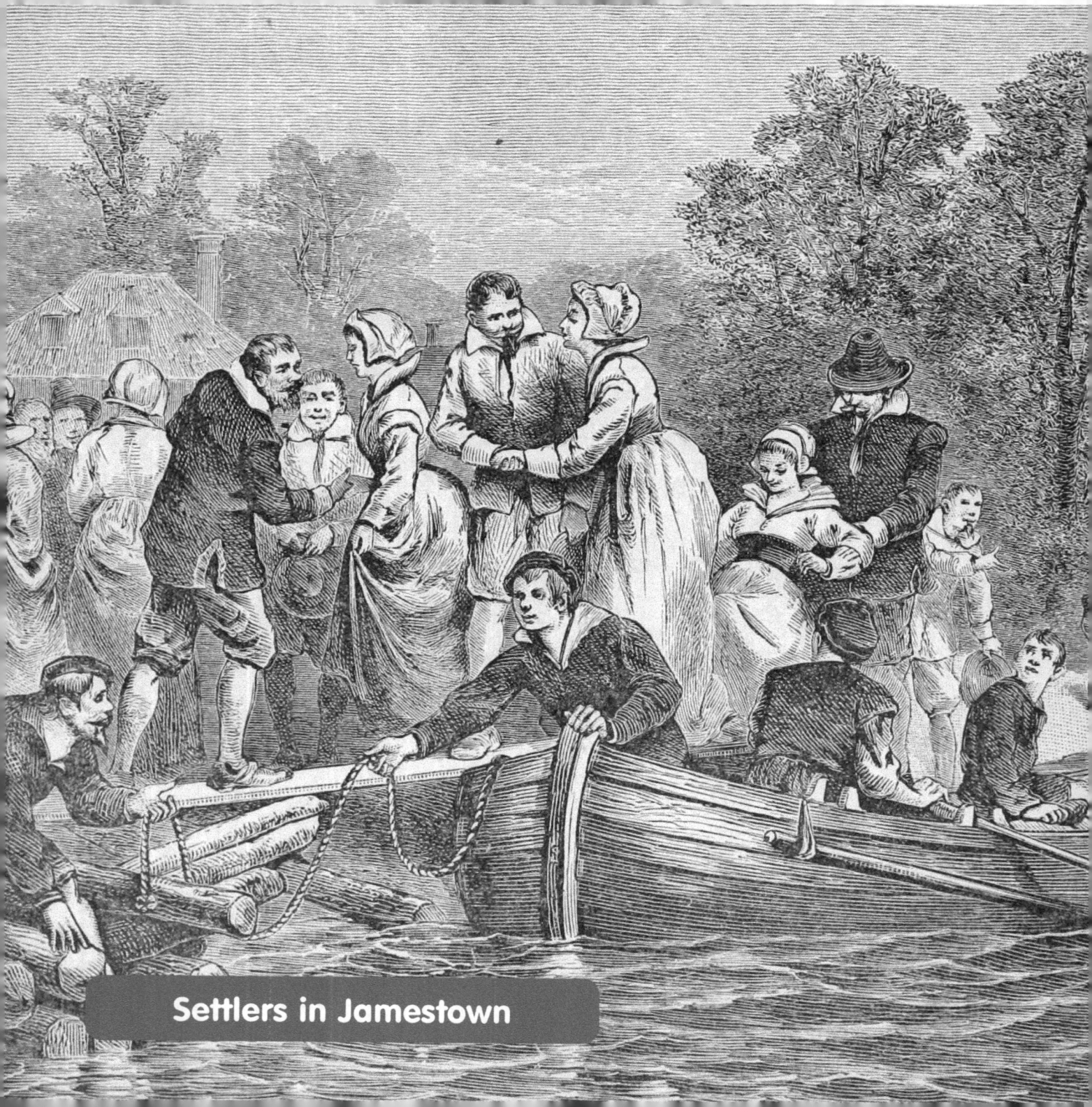

Settlers in Jamestown

THE FIRST YEAR AT JAMESTOWN

The men living in Jamestown were used to the civilized life they were living in England. They had next to no survival skills for fishing, hunting, or farming. They were living in a wilderness and weren't prepared for the harsh environment. Many of them were seeking quick riches. They thought they would find gold and return to England as wealthy men.

Because they were not prepared for the rigors of their new life, many men died the very first winter. The harsh climate coupled with diseases and the lack of food were the major reasons they perished. A few were killed by Powhatan natives. On the other hand, those who lived were helped by some of the members of the Powhatan tribes. In January, a ship with supplies helped their plight.

Powhatan Natives

CAPTAIN JOHN SMITH

In the year 1608, during the summer, Captain John Smith became the leader of the colony. Unlike the others, he was a soldier and a very experienced seaman so he was made of hardier stock than the other men. He established rules so that everyone was working to improve the colony. This made him somewhat unpopular with men who were used to sitting around letting others do the work for them. Smith sent a letter to the Virginia Company to ensure that only skilled laborers would be sent to the settlement in the future.

Captain John Smith

John Smith also wanted to establish a good relationship with the Powhatan natives. He went to visit the chief of the Powhatans, but he was captured. According to legend, he was about to be executed by the Powhatans until the chief's favorite young daughter Pocahontas saved his life. From then on, the relationship between the natives and the English settlers improved and active trading took place between the two groups.

Pocahontas saved John Smith

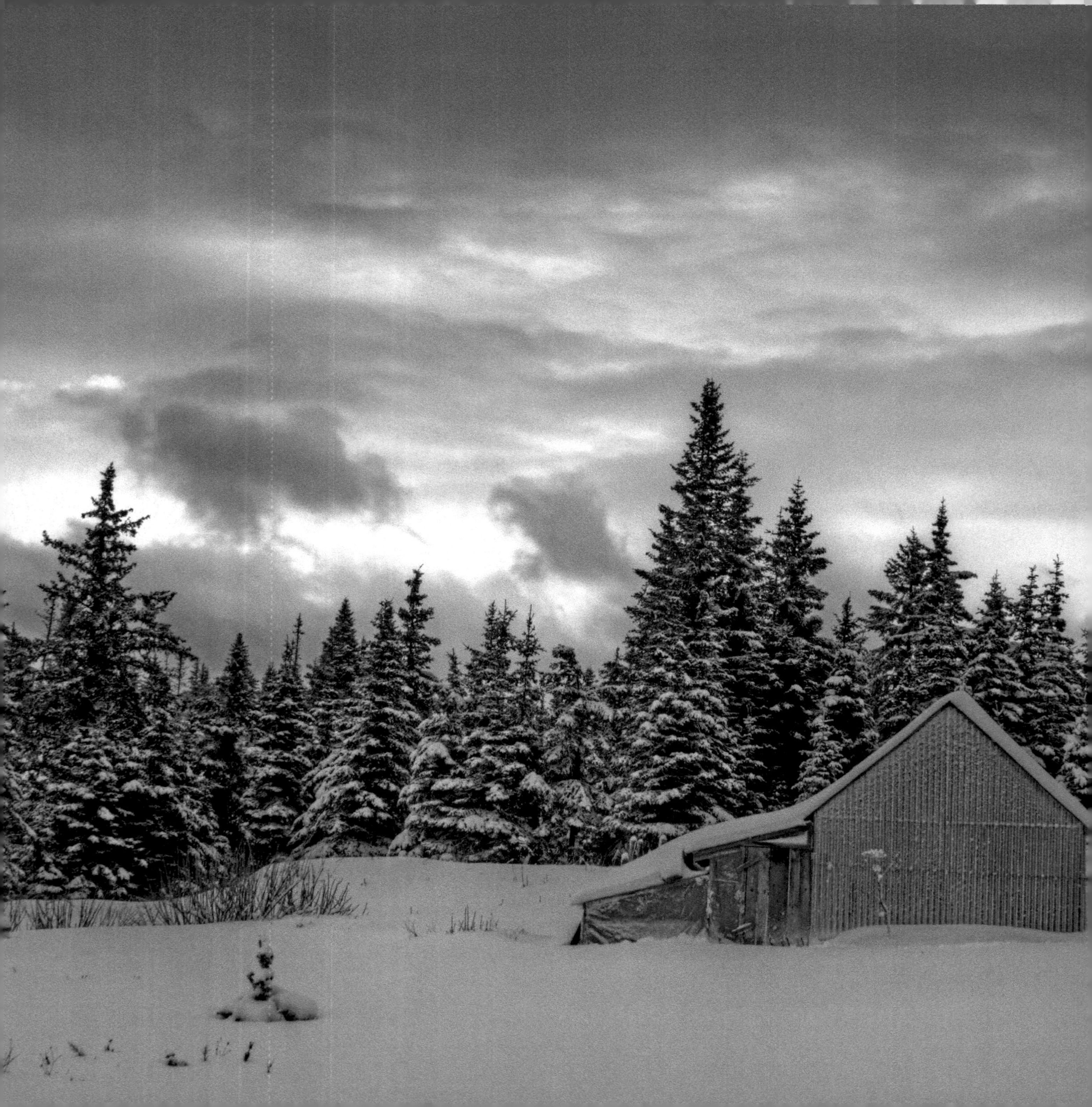

THE WINTER OF 1609 TO 1610

Captain John Smith had to return to England in 1609 because he was injured and needed medical care. Without his leadership, the colony suffered. The winter was so harsh that only 60 people survived of the 500 who were living at Jamestown at the time. The remaining group had decided to leave the colony, but when supplies arrived in the springtime they chose to stay.

JOHN ROLFE INTRODUCES TOBACCO FARMING

The colony was surviving but not thriving until John Rolfe a young farmer came to live there. He began to plant tobacco and his success with the crop began to make the settlement profitable. Eventually, John Rolfe fell in love with and married Pocahontas.

John Rolfe

Old Capitol Building and Colonial Coach

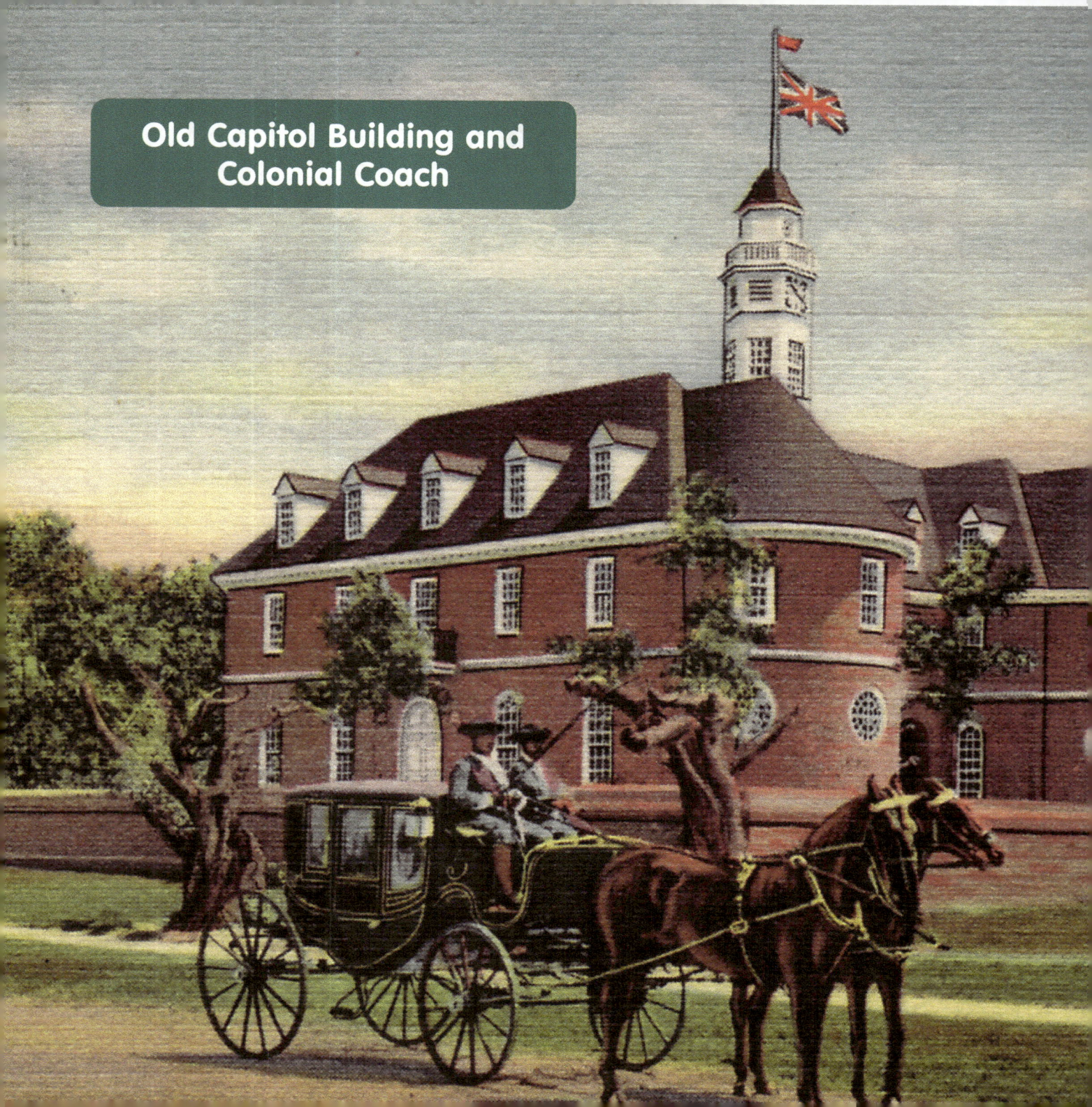

THE WILLIAMSBURG COLONY

Williamsburg quickly became an important town during colonial times. Founded in 1638 and originally named Middle Plantation, the town was only a few miles away from the Jamestown colony. Its location was far better than Jamestown since it was on higher ground and didn't become swamp-like during the summers.

Unlike Jamestown, which had not been planned, Middle Plantation was drawn out carefully before buildings were constructed. The main street was wide and the government buildings, churches, and the market square were all arranged well for public use. In 1676, after Jamestown was largely burned during an uprising called Bacon's Rebellion, the leaders of the colony decided to make Middle Plantation the capital on a temporary basis.

Bacon's Rebellion

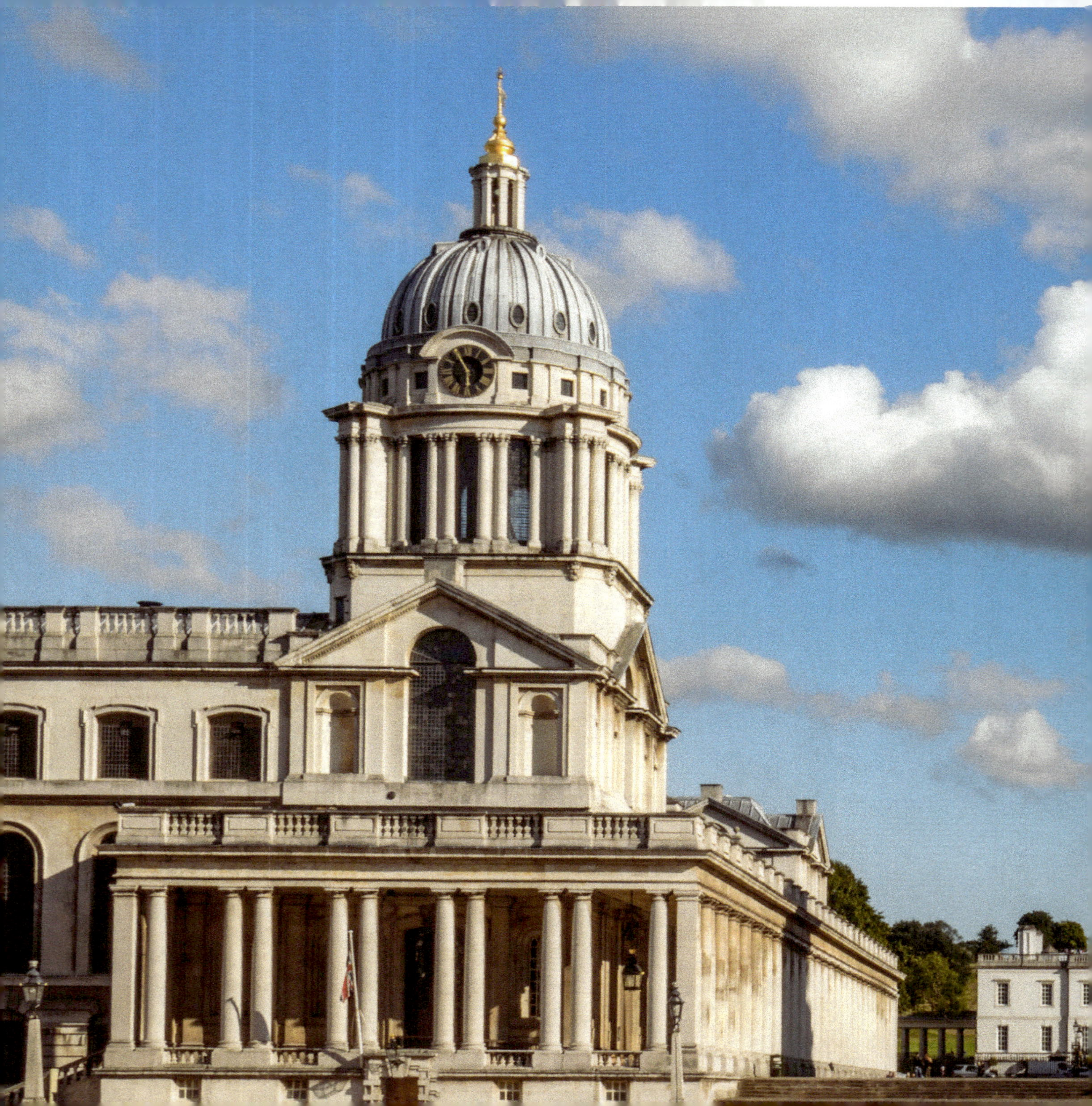

WILLIAM AND MARY COLLEGE

William and Mary College, named after England's king and queen, was founded in 1694.

It became a well-known center for learning and many American patriots were students there at one time including:

- Thomas Jefferson, the main author of the Declaration of Independence and who eventually became the third United States President
- James Monroe, who was an American statesman and became the fifth United States President
- John Marshall, who was the fourth Chief Justice of the Supreme Court
- Peyton Randolph, who was the Continental Congress's first president

James Monroe

CAPITAL OF THE VIRGINIA COLONY

When the Jamestown statehouse burned down a second time in 1698, the governing body of the colony, called the House of Burgesses, determined that the capital city should move to Middle Plantation.

Horse and carriage in Williamsburg colonial town in Virginia

The city had grown to become a political and trade center as well as a place for learning and education. They renamed the city from Middle Plantation to Williamsburg, after the king.

For a major portion of the 1700s, the city remained the capital of the colony.

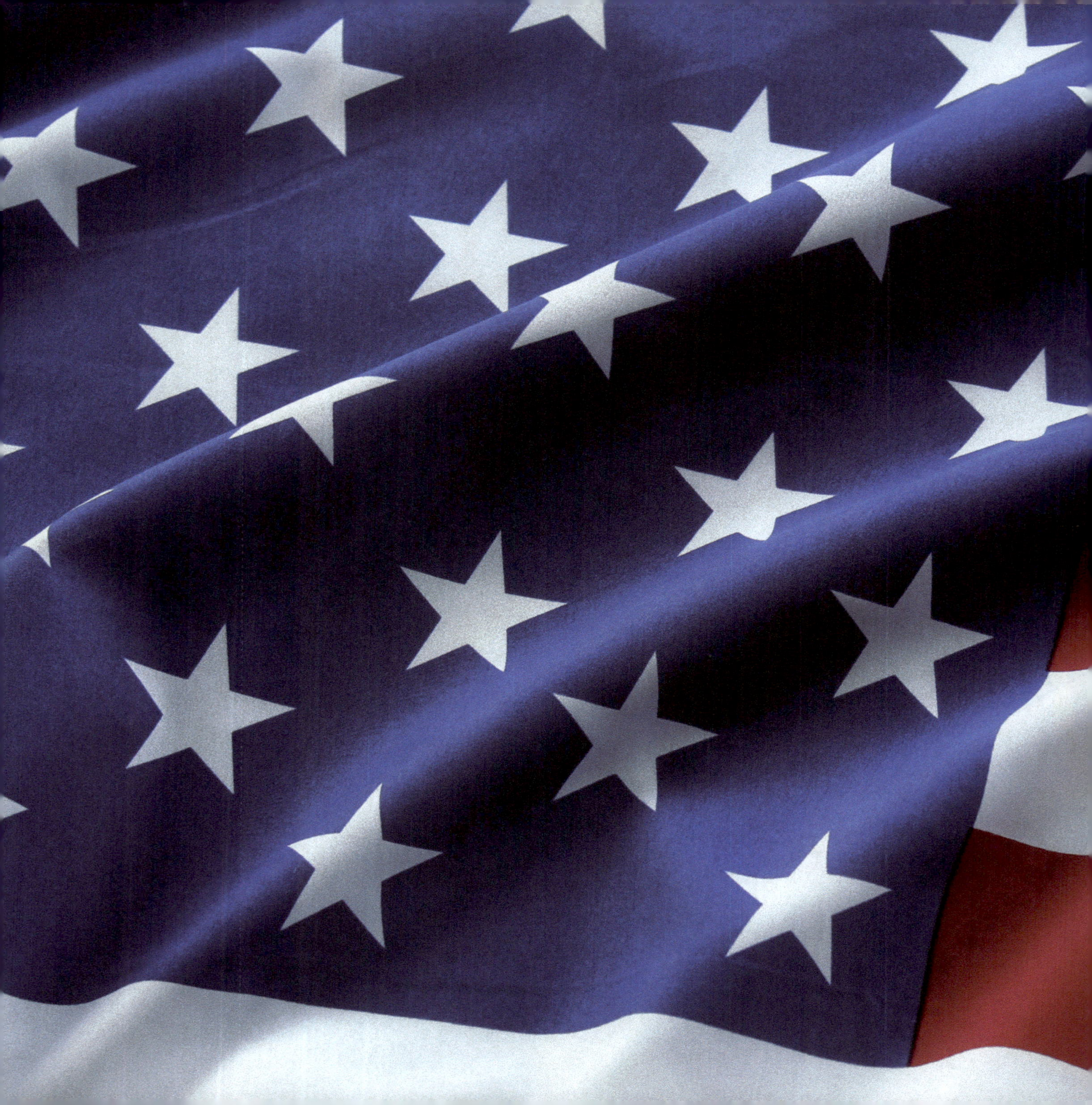

SUMMARY

When the English settlers first came to America, they weren't ready for the harsh winters, the battles with the Native Americans, and the diseases that weakened them. Many lives were lost and one colony, the colony at Roanoke, disappeared without a trace. Despite all the setbacks, from their rocky start on North America's coastline, the colonies eventually became a new country—the United States of America.

Now that you know more about the first American colonies, you can read more details about the colony of Roanoke in Baby Professor books like **The Mystery of the Lost Colony of Roanoke.**

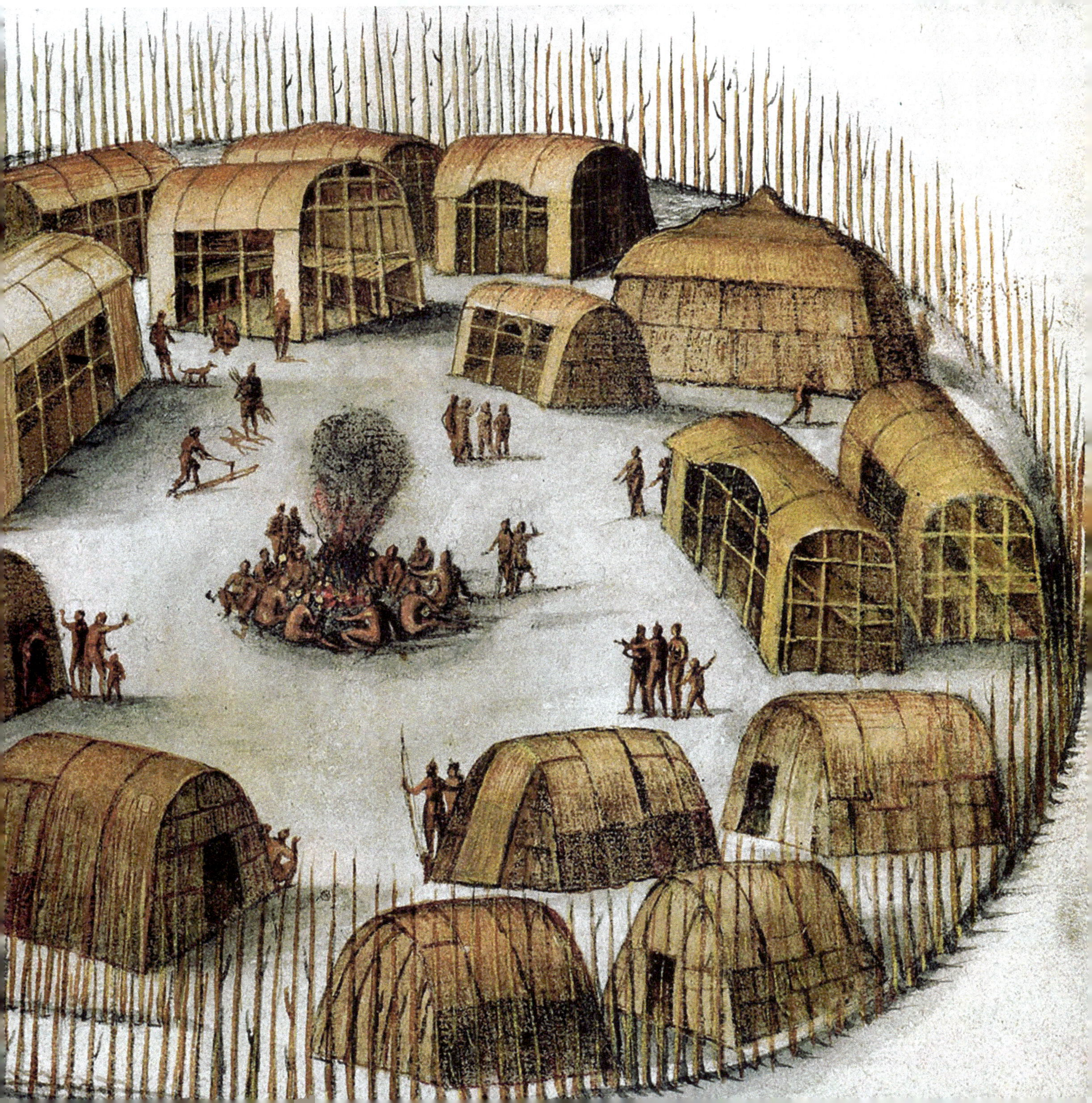

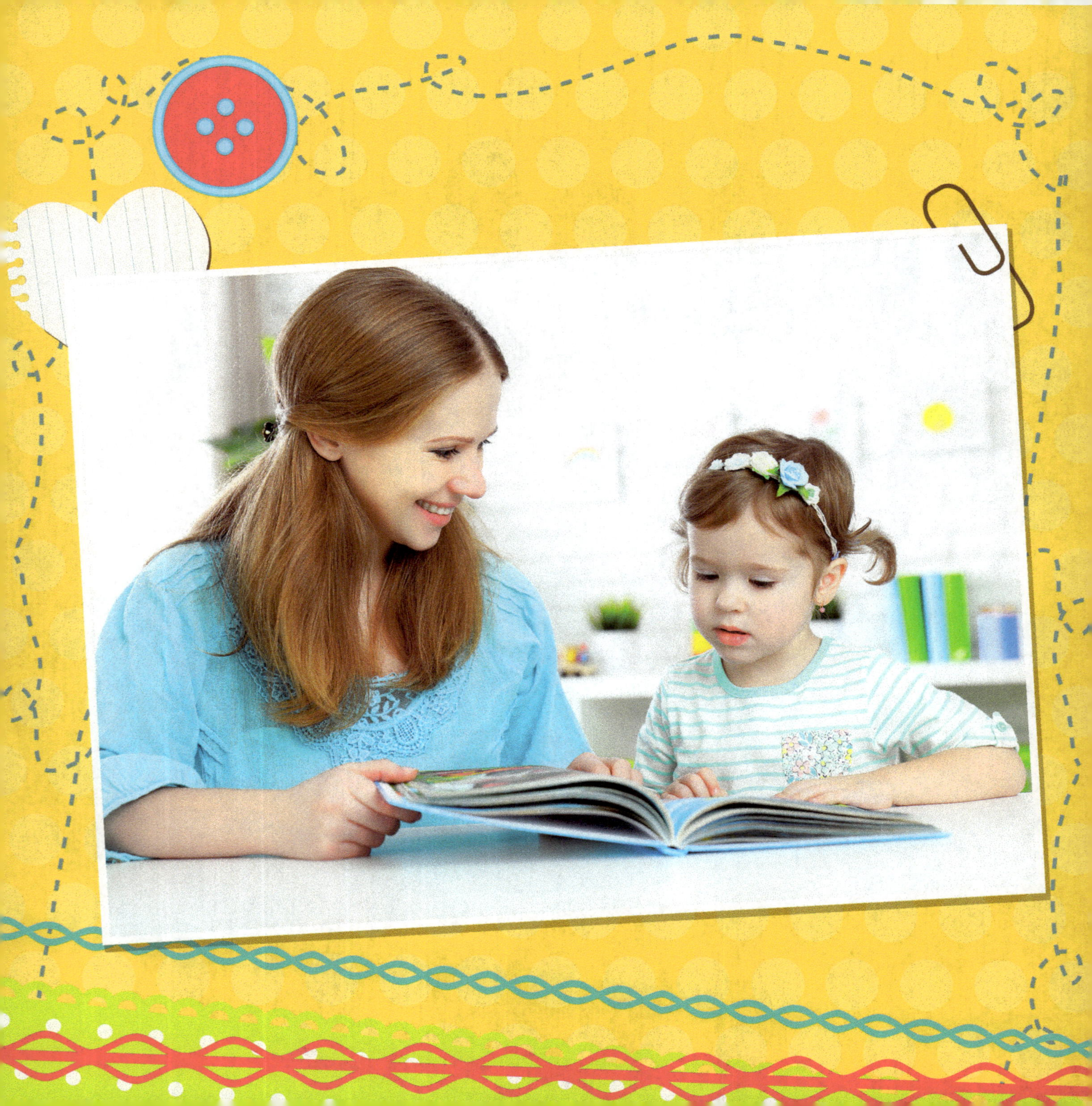

Visit

BABY PROFESSOR
EDUCATION KIDS

www.BabyProfessorBooks.com

to download Free Baby Professor eBooks
and view our catalog of new and exciting
Children's Books

Milton Keynes UK
Ingram Content Group UK Ltd.
UKHW050007300824
447530UK00002B/17

9 798869 414304